CW00358044

1 MONTH OF
FREE
READING

at

www.ForgottenBooks.com

By purchasing this book you are eligible for one month membership to ForgottenBooks.com, giving you unlimited access to our entire collection of over 1,000,000 titles via our web site and mobile apps.

To claim your free month visit:

www.forgottenbooks.com/free736746

ISBN 978-0-483-80398-5
PIBN 10736746

A STUDY OF
THINGS THE SCHOOL
SHOULD DO FOR
THE CHILD,
SUGGESTIONS ON
STUDY OF
U. S. HISTORY,
AND ARITHMETIC,
AND SOME GAINS.

BY THE STATE
SUPERINTENDENT
OF PUBLIC SCHOOLS
OF MAINE.

1902.

SOME THINGS THE COMMON SCHOOL SHOULD DO FOR THE CHILD.

It would be better for our children, and hence best for all institutions with which they are, or may be associated, if the school gave them better ideas of the relative value of facts. These stubborn things have always been with us and will remain to the end. We should, however, see clearly that isolated details are difficult to master. and when mastered, become burdens, increasing in weight as they increase in number and as we add to the length of time they are to be retained. When related and and we see this relation, they are of service, because they give us an understanding of the principles underlying them, and a conception of the teachings they embody. Unless facts illuminate or stimulate our investigations, it would be better to house them in books than in heads. If stored away in the mind, by a conscious effort, they tend to stupify and paralyze. One's information becomes a means of grace only when he knows a thing so well that he is unconscious of his knowledge. We are learning the unwisdom of trying to become wise by making ourselves walking encyclopedias. We are beginning to discover that these labors not only sap the vitality out of life, but communicate to it a certain wooden quality which takes from living its warmth, richness, power. The man who is satisfied with details grows narrower with the years and leaner as his horde increases. The miserly spirit is as surely developed by this process as it is in the poor wretch who gloats over his shining accumulations. Such a one has reached his limit of usefulness when he has told the few things he thinks he knows.

The work of the public school develops keenness of observation and skill in handling material in its student force, and hence the child comes to have an unusual facility in doing things; but the development of these powers without the safeguard of a high moral sense tends to produce rebels instead of safe citizens.

Pedagogical vagaries have taken on many forms, but perhaps the least excusable is found in the so-called enrichment of our courses of study. These additions have given us many new subjects and an almost unending list of new topics to be strained through the sieve in the top of the child's head. The result has been that the child has come to place a higher estimate on the form than on the life it shelters. He has developed great capacity for absorbing, but has not the power of digesting the facts devoured; hence, he has become the least interesting and the

most hopeless of intellectual **and** moral dyspeptics. **He suffers** from **all** the evils incident to an excessive and intoxicating diet. He has but little of that staying quality, or love for work which results from wholesome conditions. Even the physical food of the child is stimulating and irritating rather than satisfying and nourishing, while his clothing is designed to attract the attention of others and cultivate the vanity of the wearer.

Our teachers are coming to see that all questions are, in their ultimate analysis, moral questions. The age at which the child should enter school, the length of time he should remain therein, the studies he should pursue, the way in which he should do his work, the spirit which should control him, the purpose he should have in life and his willingness to serve, are among the things which should receive the first consideration but which are too often left to the decision of accident. The child can never be well taught until those having the direction of his training come to see that they are responsible for fitting a human being to become a worthy citizen of the State. Physical surroundings, mental drill, moral nurture are only useful so far as they contribute to this end.

The schools have gone much too far in directing physical action and in limiting the moral judgment of the child. His first and greatest right is the right to grow, physically and morally. The former depends upon propen and sufficient food and exercise; the latter upon counsel and guidance and also upon freedom to learn through his mistakes. If all acts are performed under external restraint. the actor is not only enfeebled, but debased. It would be better if we said less frequently "don't" and more frequently permitted the child to learn, from experience, the evils of wrong doing and the rewards of right living. Crutches are useful to the invalid, but crippling to the robust. Suggestion and even compulsion have their place in the training of the child, but if the one is used too frequently or the other is insisted upon too strenuously, the victim can neither go afoot nor alone; he can neither render a service nor increase his ability to work.

We need a saner plan for the work of the schoolroom. Intelligent thoughtfulness would teach us that facts are based upon simple principles which can be so worded as to be easily within the comprehension of the child. Facts and processes should be mastered for the purpose of making principles, not only comprehensible, but luminous. When one understands the principles involved in facts studied, he is not only growing, but is nurturing the desire for growth, and still better, is breeding the wish to give to others of the riches which flood his life and delight his soul. This better understanding not only gives zest and stimulus to work, but also develops the catholicity of spirit necessary to intelligent citizenship.

We often wonder why many of the so-called best people in the world most hinder its progress. It is largely due to the fact that they have become so absorbed in existing conditions that they are incapacitated for seeing either the genesis or the final conclusion of things. When the problem in which they are especially interested seems nearing solution they busy themselves with placing obstructions in the way of further progress.

A pupil who has been so trained that he can see that all the processes in any subject of study are based upon a few principles will grow to understand that the Ruler of the universe has an intelligent plan in the management of the world. Such enlargement of his view and powers will bring to him with controlling force the thought that much will be required of those to whom much has been given; that wherever light and virtue are found there exists the responsibility of carrying these blessings to the dwellers in darkness and to the victims of vice. The arguments in favor of expansion, as statements of facts, may or may not be convincing; the cry of imperialism, as an excuse for spasms, is of no special interest, but the principle holds, that he who has ability in large measure, is responsible for the growth of the best in others who are less fortunate. When one sees clearly the principles involved in a given course of action, then he is prepared to appreciate the moral quality of the items incident to such action and is not in danger of being blinded by a mass of details.

No school is worthy of the name unless the child taught therein comes to have a sense of his personal, community and national responsibility. This knowledge will show him that every violation of rules or laws, every instance of malicious destruction of property, every manifestation of vandalism, all exhibitions of impudence and insolence, all forms of dis-respect for persons, places, positions, sacred things, help to make possible the development of an anarchist and the evolution of an assassin. When the school shall have come into its highest estate, the child will grow to feel his accountability to himself and to that Power which has given him life that he may hasten that day for which the world is toiling, with a faith manifest in works as beautiful in spirit as they are wonderful in results.

Even the child must learn that the welfare of this Nation does not rest in the hands of its rulers, but in the lives of its common people. If this is to be a safe and a wholesome country to live in, then this multitude must come to an appreciation of the fact that true greatness consists in sim-plicity, gentleness, faithfulness, individuality, in doing our duty in the place in which we find ourselves. Station, wealth, office, name, none of these, nor all of them are necessary to the rendering of a worthy ser-vice. The child should be taught to reverence the head of a household who is true to all the interests committed to his care, and is faithful in all work his hands find to do, because he is the man who gives us the mastery, not only of the world's markets, but of its destiny as well.

It is quite as important for one to be anxious to do his work, as it is for one to work out his own salvation. The desire to walk under one's own hat; the ability to earn the hat; the capacity to do one's own reading, thinking, voting; the determination to represent one's self and count one when standing alone, are evidences of a working plan of life the world much needs in these days.

The silent as well as the oral instruction of the teacher should help the child to something better than a mastery of text-books if he is to do the work of life worthily. His schoolroom experiences should teach him that he is the sufferer as well as the loser if he makes it necessary for any one to fight for his rights, whether they be social, financial, political or religious. He can learn while yet young that failure to pay his proportion of the public assessment of service or tax is a crime against himself and one for which he will find it difficult to atone. He will here have opportunities to learn that he is not only doing the right thing but promoting all his best interests when he seeks to give to others equal or better opportunities than have fallen to his own lot.

The wisest man since Plato has said: "There are a thousand who can talk for one who can think, and a thousand more who can think for one who can feel; for to feel is poetry, philosophy, and religion all in one." No school can assist in fitting a child for life unless it leads him to see that it is as necessary for him to feel a truth as to know what is true. There can be no question but that feeling is the highest form of intelligence yet discovered by the subtlest psychologist. Our great poets have been, not only the historians of the future, but have also lived most because they have loved most. The thrilling pulse of nature has startled them with its power; the wisdom embalmed in the daisy has taught them of life, death and the judgment to come; they have read the record written in the rocks because they have been in touch as well as in tune with Nature.

The child has a right to look to the teacher for light and guidance. It is his privilege to stand between the masters and the child and with an expression more halting, render it possible for him to make companions of these great souls and drink of the fountains which they, like Longfellow's Pegasus, have left for the refreshment of all who will drink.

It was not the learning of Mark Hopkins, the wisdom of Dr. Arnold, nor the vision of Horace Mann, that made each a power while living and a blessing in these latter days, but it was the fact that they possessed in fullest measure that fine appreciation of life in all its forms which found its highest manifestation in old Domsie. This love of art and of the child made that old stone schoolhouse in the Glen among the pines more than a university and kept Domsie on the watch for the boy o'parts and gave him a sagacity which made it easy to provide ways and means to send the youth, when found, to Edinboro.

The child is entitled to such an introduction to the masters as will enable him to understand the stations into which they were born, the conditions under which they worked, the sufferings they endured and the service they rendered. To him the lives of Wagner, Millet, Michæl Angelo and Lincoln must be something more than dates and names and places. He must appreciate the humble homes into which three of them were born, and the noble parentage of the fourth, and he must be able to discern, as his acquaintance with them becomes more intimate, that each loved some form of nature with a great passion; that each had a purpose to which he was true through appalling sufferings; that each sweat great drops of blood that other lives might be better lived, and that each opened the windows of the souls of millions and let in the light of truth and beauty. This acquaintanceship should be promoted until the child is able to pass his hand within the arm of one of the saviors of the race and go with him down the long path which leads to the haven of all good. While on one of these pilgrimages his cheeks will be aglow, and his eyes will shine with the light that glorifies the face of the devout peasant when he gazes enraptured on the masterpieces of Raphael.

He must learn while yet young, that there are two atmospheres in this world; the one is physical and fills our lungs; the other is spiritual and gives new and better life to our souls. The first serves its purpose in the act which makes use of it; the second remains with us through all time. It comes to us through seers and prophets, making the divine manifest in human life.

He must be so taught and must so train himself that he can walk in Elysian fields, through jasper gates, along golden streets; kneel at the great white throne, and see sights never revealed to mortal eyes, because he has that vision which the imagination, warmed by sympathy, can bring to him of the Paradise seen by John Milton and the Pilgrim created by John Bunyan.

The right reading of the thirty-eighth chapter of Job, the nineteenth, twenty-third and ninetieth Psalms, the twelfth chapter of Ecclesiastes, the fifty-third chapter of Isaiah, the fifth chapter of Daniel, the Sermon on the Mount, the fourteenth chapter of the Gospel of St. John, the thirteenth chapter of First Corinthians, and the twenty-first chapter of Revelations, will help him to see something of the power and wisdom of God as well as His love for His children, and will permit him to trace in his ancestors the pathways he has traveled and to catch glimpses of that undiscovered country toward which he is journeying.

The child has a right to know quite as much of the Christ who was born in a stable, cradled in a manger, who lived in a peasant's cottage, worked at a carpenter's bench, who was so poor that he had not where to lay his head, and yet was heard gladly by the common people because he brought light and life into the world, as he is required to learn of the unsavory details of the gods of so-called heathen nations.

It would be well from the pedagogical standpoint if our teachers sat at the feet of the Great Teacher of Nazareth and learned some of the simple, homely lessons of daily life. Such instruction would make it impossible for them to devote so much time to the evils of wrong doing, and would induce them to win the child to a better life by showing him the blessings which come from righteous living. It would make them more hospitable toward truth wherever found, whether it be in the heart of a child or the teachings of the sage. It would give that kind of courage which would cast out all fear, except that which comes from the dread of being a coward. They would learn that it is not a difficult matter and not often an important item for one to have opinions, but it is vital that he be controlled by convictions, otherwise he will be carried into devious and dangerous paths by the foolish teachings of the unwise. They would discover how to become rich without wealth, and happy without luxury. Under these influences the whisperings of the message of the spirit will be heard while the clamor of its physical embodiment will be but little heeded. They will grow so sensitive for others that they will have no time to be sensitive for themselves. They will come to know that life is alive as long as it is used to give life to others. They will see that the world needs to-day, more than ever before, not the arrogance of knowledge, but the graciousness of culture. That above all, and giving the motive to all, will be the faith that the love which cleanses the lover will purify the world.

The school will help the child as it makes it possible for him to grow, to master himself and his tasks, to feel the pulse of nature, to live in close communion with the wise of heart, to rejoice in the companionship of those who have pointed the way, and gone on before, to receive truth and embalm it in daily living, and to be glad to be alone with God in his own heart.

A nation born in righteousness must live righteously. The menace of to-day is not ignorance, but the lack of a controlling moral sentiment. We cannot endure as a people if we place a higher estimate on learning than we accord to virtue. The time has come when we would better teach less cube root and devote more attention to the fundamental principles of right living. That training of the will which keeps us in the right path is more to be desired than the wisdom found in books. That school serves the child best which helps him to do instinctively the right thing, to feel approval for the act done, and at the same time, to have an intelligent understanding of the issues involved.

The school that does this work gives to all organizations that are seeking to make good things better the help they have a right to demand.

SOME SUGGESTIONS ON THE STUDY OF UNITED STATES HISTORY.

It is the rule rather than the exception that we attempt to learn of our Nation's history by trying to master the dates and facts that make up the record of this continent since 1492. Such efforts always have been and will continue to be, in a measure, futile. Our history goes back to the beginning of time. No one can understand American life who is not familiar with the record made by our ancestors on English shores. No one can study English history to advantage unless he is familiar with the story of the Northmen, the Normans, the Angles, Saxons, Jutes and Frisians. The two great classic nations have also had much to do with moulding our thought and modifying our lives. It is easy to see that our history begins with a day too early to be fixed with exactness.

Some six or sixty or six hundred thousand years ago, there lived in central western Asia, or somewhere else, a small community, springing from a common ancestor, and having kindred tastes, characteristics, aptitudes and occupations. As years went on, differences arose, varying capacities were evolved, desires for new fields to conquer were born, and ambitions to found other and separate communities were developed. Those having interests in common gathered themselves together into clans, septs, bands or tribes, and leaving their early homes, went their several ways, and in process of time grew to be the nations of the earth.

One section found its way south and east and became the ancestors of the unnumbered millions of India. They were in those early days, and have remained through all the years, meditative, introspective, metaphysical. They have dreamed dreams and seen visions; they have been the authors of a great literature and the fathers of subtle philosophy. The Western mind has spun no thread so fine that these keen-eyed Orientals have not found it easy to separate it into two sections, and with a nicety which does not permit us to discover which is the larger part. These dwellers in far eastern lands are full brothers of ours and have exerted an influence on our lives in the past, and are to be more influential in our living in the future, and hence the necessity for our knowing somewhat concerning them.

The Celts seem to have been the second division to make their way out into the unknown world, and we find them in the Basques of Spain, the native Gauls of France, the Welsh in Wales, the Manx in the Isle of Man, the Irishry of Ireland, and the native Picts and Scots. They were largely endowed with fancy and imagination. They furnished the yeast for the human race. They were warmed by the genial rays of joy and withered by the blasts of sorrow. They responded to the artistic and poetic— to beauty wherever found. They had that warmth and unthinking impulsiveness which made them the football of the world for centuries.

The Greeks found their way into the islands of the Aegean and the valleys of the most beautiful peninsula of all the earth. They were the lovers and embodiers of beauty. They saw it in the hills about them, the valleys at their feet, the winding stream, the changing cloud, and gave expression to it in grove and temple, in oration and poem, in painting and statue. Beauty was their god, and at its shrine they worshipped and in this devotion we are blessed.

The Romans found a home in another and more western peninsula. They were born to rule and brought the then known world under their domination. They devised and administered a central government. Much of our civil law and many of our civil forms come from this early people. They were possessed of dignity, that peculiar self-respect which made the humblest Roman a king and fit to rule the peers of the realm.

The Teutons found their way into northwestern Europe. They lived among fogs and fens, bogs and morasses. They were coarse, brutal savages. They were passionate lovers and fiercest haters. They were gluttons in eating and sots in drinking. They loved home, women, kindred, liberty, and took pride in each man representing himself, defending his own rights and performing his own duties. They had that inherent strength, sturdiness, endurance, absorbing faculties which made it possible for them to take in all of good other nations evolved, make it their own and add to it the saving qualities which they themselves possessed, i. e., the ability to multiply their virtues and rid themselves of their vices.

There are two divisions of the race of which mention has not been made. One filled a large place in the past and the other is to fill a world-wide place in the future. The Slav had not a little of the metaphysical twist of the East Indian, a large endowment of the love of the beautiful inherent in the Greek, the masterful qualities possessed by the Roman, the staying powers given in such large measure to the Teuton and the exalted and exulting forces so regnant in the old Celt. A strain of Tartar blood poisoned the current of his life for a long time and gave to his national existence a barbaric trend and an oriental flavor. The years have come and gone, the winnowing process has been carried on, the Clock of Time is about to strike. The Slav of to-day, as manifest in the Russian of the present, is to dispute the conquest of the world with his western brothers, the assertive Englishman and the still more presumptuous American.

The Hebrew, living on the hills and in the orchards of Judea, had for his mission the development of a moral code. This work he performed with that peculiar wisdom which makes evident the special direction of an over-ruling hand.

One of the strange lessons to be drawn from all these facts, is that four of these divisions seem to have had a special mission to perform and a particular problem to solve. The Hebrews gave us a formal statement of our relation to the God we worship; the Greeks gave us our capacity to love the beautiful; the Romans gave us the power to rule; the Celts have sent through our veins, in hot currents, those vivid imaginings so necessary to sane living, whether the life be that of the statesman, the toiler upon the sea, the laborer upon the land, the priest in his cloister, or the poet in his study. It is easy to note that these peoples lived isolated lives, and in this isolation they toiled and thus were able to serve. To each, all others were heathen and foes to be feared, or enemies to be slain. It is not possible for a teacher to give instruction in American history unless she knows much of the swing and trend, relation and purpose of all these peoples.

Another method might be used in bringing the facts of the past before the mind of the child in striking form. Two thousand years ago Rome ruled the world and peace prevailed to its utmost borders, and Christ was born among the hills of Judea. He came to bring peace and good-will to all mankind. Five hundred years come and go, and Rome with-draws from northwestern Europe and retires within narrow limits. The tribes of Germany over-run England and drive into the hills the native Britons. The Vandals conquer southern Europe and carry their devas-tations to the shores of the Mediterranean and the Empire transfers its throne to the Bosphorus. Another five hundred years pass away, and the Normans have conquered England; America has been discovered; the Albigenses' Reformation has spread its flickering and short-lived light over central western Europe. Another five hundred years have been rolled up in the scroll, and with it have come the invention of printing and of gunpowder, the rediscovery of America, the Lutheran reformation, the revival of learning, the crumbling of the Eastern Empire, and the dis-persion of Greek learning and literature throughout western Europe.

It is easy to see that events swing in great cycles in the world's supreme movements. There seems to be an ebb and flow in the affairs of men which leave great determining facts standing out like the high mountain peaks in our loftiest ranges. The skillful teacher can give the child such bird's-eye views of this great current of human life that its essential facts may stand revealed to him in the clear, white light of truth.

We have seen that there was a fountain, far away in eastern lands from which many streams have flowed in diverse and diverging directions. It is no figure of speech to say that all these great rivers have converged and found their last reservoir this side of the Atlantic. To us have come all nations and all peoples, each laden with his burden, each bringing his contribution. The amalgamation of all these elements will, in the end, give us the ideal citizen of the world. We are to have, in the days that are to come, that fine reverence and devotion for which the Jew strove but never attained. We are to have the sensuous enjoyment of beauty without any of the sensualism which characterized the early Greek. We are to be strong enough, one of these days, to rule more wisely than the Roman ever ruled, because we shall govern without tyranny. We are to have the vision which enabled the ancient Celt to see radiant vistas. We shall have all these things because the underlying and essential part of our inheritance comes from that portion of the race that is possessed of the power which makes it easy for them to absorb the good and reject the evil which life offers.

Nothing could be more unwise than for the common school teacher to spend her time trying to gain information concerning those peoples by studying the heavy tomes of which Rawlinson's is, perhaps, the best example. This information can be most easily gathered from anecdote, incident, sketch, story, tradition, legend. Butterworth, Miss Yonge, Bolton, Knox will furnish world portraits and pictures, while Mahaffy and the Story of the Nation Series will give her a truer historical per-spective and a better basis for future study. The child should be made to see the homes these people builded, the schools they maintained, the temples in which they worshipped, the industries with which they occupied themselves; in a word, to come in touch with the daily life of the common people, know the leaders and breathe the atmosphere created by the good and great. He must walk adown the long path with an Indian mystic and let him tell the story of his people; go with an old Greek out into the groves and stand beneath its arching trees, or sit in the porches of one of those noble temples and listen to the gracious wisdom of a sage; live again in the City that sat on seven hills and discover how it ruled the world; stand by some Druidical circle, and watch the weird rites with which the old Celt propitiated his gods; find a home beneath the lowering skies of that old Germany which has given us the brain that holds in charge so large a share of the world's activities. The old world in all its interests, all its hopes and fears, all its aspirations and shortcomings, must live again in the child's fertile imagination, and all classes, conditions, sects, races, must be known by him through that medium which teaches history better than the formal record has ever given it to us.

If we come more definitely within the limits of our own history it is well for us to take note of the two great classes which made early settlements within our borders. The Pilgrim and the Puritan are our ancestors; the Cavalier found a home beneath warmer skies. The Puritan was cold, brusque, harsh, enjoyed suffering for the good he felt it wrought within him. He was severe in his judgment of himself and cruel in his relations to others, but he was strong and clean and righteous, faithful and hardy and earnest; did his own reading and his own thinking, and braced himself to fight oppression wherever manifested. The Cavalier was refined without being scholarly; he had polish, grace and an easy observance of conventional forms. He gloried in broad acres, baronial homes, and many of the trappings of royalty. He was eager, ardent, impulsive, a thorough-going hater, and a friend loyal to his last dollar and his last drop of blood. Separated by an imperceptible line, these two classes waxed strong, multiplied in numbers, advanced in civilization and contended for supremacy. The Cavalier yielded to the yeoman. In yielding, he received much of blessing and gave richly of the quality most needed in Northern life—that fine observance of the amenities of modern society, so necessary to civil and civilized living. If these outlines are clearly set before the child, he can see the Southern home and the Northern fireside; the broad stretching fields of Virginia and the smaller homestead of New England; the self-contained power of the one and the over-flowing spirits of the other, and this knowledge will help him to truer ideas of the sources from which he came, the inheritance which is his and the responsibilities placed upon him.

The child should also have opportunities to study persons, places and events. He should study the individual in such a way that he will know of his ancestry, home, childhood, young manhood, mature years, the training he received, the tasks to which he gave himself, the work he did, the results coming from it. This study should make *Samuel Adams* something more than a name to him. This rare old Puritan, living in a quiet home, on a secluded street, cared for by his wife, made possible the Revolution and its successful issue. He was the one man who saw the conflict long before it came, hastened its coming, effected the consolidation of the Colonies, held John Hancock in all his limpness to his task and place, and fought the intellectual battles of this great war. Samuel Adams was the supreme mind of his day;—large enough to be willing to keep out of sight, strong enough to use the means which came to his hand, and true enough to fight it out on the line chosen if it took a hundred summers.

The Missouri Compromise is an event which should be treated with a fullness not possible in a half dozen lines of an ordinary text-book. It was the crucial point in our history; toward it all details led; from it all subsequent history radiates. It was the beginning of the end of a struggle centuries old, and it also made possible our present commanding position. It is the pivot around which revolve a hundred lesser questions in the settlement of which came the final decision declared by Lincoln to be inevitable.

Valley Forge is a place that should be sacred to every lover of liberty. Here men stood and suffered, and served as they waited. Here men's souls were tried, and here it was determined that if eternity should be needed to settle the question of the freedom of the Colonies, eternity should be dedicated to that holy purpose.

A comprehensive idea of our Civil War may be given through the use of a simple illustration. Place the edge of the hand upon the map with the thumb upward and the wrist resting just below the city of Washington, extend the hand across Virginia and West Virginia and over into Kentucky, and allow the fingers to follow down the Mississippi river, and as they close in, come across Georgia, Alabama, and the Carolinas, and when the ends of the fingers have come back to the wrist, you have the circumference of the rebellion and you have the life squeezed out of the conspiracy. The strong strain was, at the start, and remained to the end of the war, at the wrist, and it is here the greatest power was resident. Hard fighting came along through the back of the hand; the gathering into the crushing folds of the fingers indicates the battles fought on the Gulf. It is an illustration that seems to be helpful in making clear to the child the seat of the conflict, the extent of the disaffection, and the efforts made to reduce the rebelling states to subjection.

It is evident that these suggestions have covered a wide area, set a swift pace, outlined work for whose mastery years would be insufficient. Still it cannot be denied that it is necessary for us to know the point at which we started, the highways we have traveled, the places we have reached, the direction in which we are facing, the goal which is destined to be ours if we are true to ourselves and loyal to the best within us.

There is no question but that our language and literature, industries and civilization, homes and churches, schools and philanthropies, are to go to the ends of the earth and the islands of the sea. Wherever darkness is found, there the light set beneath these western skies must shed its beams, or the vice and the degradation which lurks in these far away places will become the agents of our undoing. Great blessings are ours; these can only remain our choicest possession by giving them to those who stand in need of the best the ages have given us.

ARITHMETIC IN THE COMMON SCHOOLS.

All children have limitations. Some have meagre possibilities. Any attempt to compel a child to do work he cannot comprehend results in arrested development. He not only remains a stranger to the subject studied, but he loses the ability to understand and use what he could otherwise have made helpfully his own. A few children are debarred by nature from receiving scholastic training beyond a certain point. It is the duty of the school to aid such in pursuing their studies as far as possible. The generations yet to come must take the succeeding steps in the advancement of this portion of the race. Other children are unable, because of immaturity, to study with profit certain branches during their early years. All efforts tending to force these studies upon them result in benumbing not only the powers used, but in paralyzing all the faculties of the mind. One child in many thousands seems to be able to assimilate all kinds of intellectual food at every period of his development. He is the exception and is but little helped or harmed by the school. . The majority of children must be taught intelligently if our schools are to provide us with useful citizens. They must have a chance to learn the things they can learn at the time they can master them best and above all, they must acquire those things which, in the learning, will give them the most power and will provide them with a store of usable information and thus make it possible for them to live wisely, safely and helpfully.

The work of teaching can never be well done until the teacher understands the child, has mastered the subjects studied, knows modern methods so thoroughly that she uses them unconsciously, is capable of inventing her own devices, and has a well defined idea of the results she wishes to accomplish. That some of these conditions do not exist, and that none of them are as much in evidence as thoughtful students of the educational problem desire, go without saying. That we are steadily, if not rapidly, making improvements along these lines is also manifest.

The fatal weakness at the present time is our ignorance of the child. The so-called Child Study so extensively advertised during the past few years has furnished not a little amusement to the profession and much entertainment for the general public. It has thus far done but little to make the work of the teacher more effective. It has not, as yet, furnished sufficient justification for the time devoted to these studies and their exploitation.

No elaborate experiments nor subtle psychological investigations are needed to convince the intelligent teacher of the justness of the following statements. The child's mental powers should be trained during the period of their greatest natural activity. Any attempt to compel him to study a large number of subjects at a given time, or to swamp him in details, or to insist that he shall understand principles when he can best master facts, or to ask him to do many of the things now required in our common schools, will be attended with results lamented by so many teachers. The stupifying of the child so taught will surely follow.

It is apparent to any observer that in his early years the child is eager in his questionings and alert in his observations. The work of the schools should help him to put his questions in intelligent form and obtain from his observations a reasonably definite knowledge of the objects within the range of his vision. During this period, nature, music, pietorial art, reading, penmanship, spelling and a limited amount of number work, illustrated by familiar objects, may be studied with pleasure and profit. The age when these studies may be pursued to the best advantage varies with different pupils, but speaking generally it includes those of the primary grades.

During the next period the child collects and records. At this time the head and pockets are filled with all kinds of material. He is a repository and a magazine and, in a limited sense, a cyclopedia. Facts have great attraction for him. He memorizes easily. He is willing to drudge in making his collections and rejoices as he sees his accumulations multiply. He should be so trained in all the combinations he will ever have occasion to use, that as soon as the items are named, the result will be present in his mind. Whenever he sees the expression eight plus seven, plus five, he will think the number *twenty* as readily as he thinks of the word *cat* when he sees the letters c a t. He should be required to memorize definitions, rules, literary gems, selections and certain general facts in the several subjects studied. The arithmetical part of this work should be made intelligible by the use of illustrations taken from his daily experiences. The work outlined in this paragraph can be done best during the intermediate grades.

Having been taught to question intelligently, observe with discrimination, retain with definiteness and accuracy, he is prepared for the next step in his progress.

In the last three years of the common school course he is fitted to contrast, compare, infer, in a word, to reason. He can now address himself to the subject matter and science of arithmetic. He should be required to apply facts to the illustration of principles. He has reached a point in his development where he can see the truths underlying the rule given, the definition recited and the problem solved. He will have less concern about getting the "right answer" and more interest in mastering the thought expressed. He will be able to comprehend and apply those fundamental principles in arithmetic so little understood even by some teachers.

The following illustrations are so familiar as not to need elaboration and are therefore stated in their simplest terms. Addition is counting on by ones and multiplication is counting on by twos, threes, etc.; subtraction is taking from by ones and division is taking from by twos, threes, etc.; hence addition and multiplication are counting *on* and subtraction and division are counting *from*. Stated in its simplest form, these four fundamental rules include the entire process of counting. As the pupil goes forward in his work, he will discover that the following problem involves the most important principles dealt with in this branch of study. If a man buy four cows for $100.00, what will five cows cost? When he shall have made his own all the facts and principles contained in the above propositions, he will have a mastery of more of the science of arithmetic than is possessed by the average graduate of our common schools.

One of these days we shall be wise enough to limit the work in arithmetic to the four fundamental rules, common fractions, decimals, the simple applications of denominate numbers and percentage. This work will be illustrated and rendered helpful in mental training by using material which the child collects, and using it in such a way as to make valuable his every day experiences with his schoolmates, his home and other associates. We shall be content to leave involution, evolution, alligation, permutations, foreign exchange, annual interest and the finding of the solid contents of the frustum of a pyramid for later years, and sometimes we shall be wise enough to leave them for years that will never arrive.

It is questioned if many people appreciate the amount of time devoted to, or wasted, upon arithmetic. The child commences this branch when he enters school and, in most cases, devotes at least one whole period each day for five days in the week during all the years he remains in the primary, intermediate and grammar grades. This simple statement brings home with tremendous force the waste made by the child in the time given to this subject. It also reveals the extent of our stumbling in the twilight of things.

Any one familiar with the work and with the young child's inability to master it, knows that if he commence it at a later date, when his mental training fits him for the task, three years make possible a comprehension of the subject that nine years of drudgery under present methods fail to give. Stated in another form, the child who devotes his eighth and ninth years to a mastery of number in simple combinations, his tenth and eleventh years to learning something about definitions and rules and the simple processes involved, and his twelfth and thirteenth years to the study of arithmetic, will make a great saving in time and acquire a knowledge of the subject possessed by few adults.

The natural inferences to be gathered from the foregoing discussion are included in the following statement. We would do better work if we commenced the study later, devoted less time to it, mastered the fundamental facts, understood the essential principles, applied them to the ordinary experiences of life, and omitted a large portion of the text which now furnishes puzzles and the study of which produces stupefaction. If we could fully realize the injury inflicted upon the child by the amount of work we require of him, the unnaturalness of his attempt to understand intricate and abstruse reasoning processes in his early years, and the comparatively rare use ever made of the knowledge acquired, then we would give to this branch the time it merits and get out of it the mental training it is capable of giving.

It is hardly necessary to say that while doing the work indicated above, the child should receive such instruction in art, literature, geography, history and other subjects as will furnish opportunities for the development of his imagination and the culture of his sympathies; such nurture as will put him in touch and tune with life in all its best forms.

We shall, one of these days, see the unwisdom of sending the child to school when he is five years of age. The historian of the future will furnish in proof of our semi-civilized state, the fact that we did not allow the child his first and greatest right, the right to grow. Before many years, the age when the child may enter school will be raised to six; later, will be advanced to seven and before the present century closes, will be fixed at eight years. The years now devoted to the primary grades will be given to a modified form of kindergarten training. This work will be so administered that the child will become sturdy physically, intelligent and responsive morally, and alert and ambitious intellectually. Then we shall not see the limpness and indifference manifest in so many children. They will be allowed to start at the beginning, go forward in the paths in which they are fitted by nature to walk, and in the end acquire that power which natural conditions and wholesome work, pursued according to intelligent methods, can give them.

These changes are not to be made at once and it is not best that radical means be adopted in bringing them about, but all who are interested in the training of our youth, and especially our school officials and teachers, should give to the problem stated above, such reading, study, investigation and prudent experiment as will, in a reasonable time, replace the methods found in our common schools with such school privileges as will permit the child to be the most his capacities and abilities will allow him to become.

SOME GAINS.

That there has been an increasingly intelligent administration of our schools during the past few years admits of no question. Parents are insisting that efficient teachers be placed in charge of the instruction of their children; that school officials discharge the duties devolving upon them with the faithfulness which characterizes the methods used by the prudent individual in the management of his private affairs; and above all, they are assisting by their personal efforts and gifts, in making the school grounds more attractive and in supplying the schoolrooms with books and pictures for the use, not only of the teachers and pupils, but also of the people of the community in which the school is located. School officials are also making studies of school sanitation; are urging towns to make improvements in out-buildings and school-buildings; are exercising greater care in purchasing material, and are calling for teachers who are scholastically and professionally fitted to render acceptable service in the schoolroom. Teachers are attending Teachers' Institutes and Summer Schools in larger numbers than ever before. They show the liveliest interest in learning the best methods of instruction, and they are providing themselves with the latest books on pedagogy and the most useful magazines on schoolroom work. Even the children seem to have caught the spirit which so largely influences those who are striving to improve our common schools. Nearly fifty-five thousand members have been enrolled in the School Improvement Leagues of Maine. The work done by this organization is valuable because of the results accomplished, but is still more useful in that it is developing a local interest in the local school, which in time will result in making it the social, literary and art center of the community in which it is located. Hundreds of school yards have been graded and converted into lawns, and trees, shrubs and flowers have been planted in a number so large that the figures seem almost incredible. Tumbled-down fences have been replaced by those of more attractive patterns. Out-buildings that were a moral menace to the children have been burned, and others of improved construction have been built in their places. A large number of school-buildings have been painted, and the ceilings and walls of scores of schoolrooms have been papered or tinted. The list of materials furnished through the efforts of the members of the League is too long to be enumerated at this time. It includes many thousand volumes of books, a still larger number of pictures, globes, maps, charts and other apparatus, and utensils without number. The organization has been in existence a little more than three years. Its work has been so far-reaching that it has practically produced a revolution in many communities.

SOME CONDITIONS.

While great gains have been made, it is clear that a larger work remains to be performed than has yet been accomplished. It is true that parents, school officials, teachers and pupils are working together for the betterment of our schools with an energy and efficiency never before seen in this State, yet it is also true that certain things must be done before our schools can properly serve the children. Each succeeding decade places larger responsibilities upon the shoulders of those who have come upon the stage of action than fell to the lot of their predecessors. To be able to do this work with credit to themselves and for the greatest good of those for whom it is done, the doers must have the best blood, nurture, environment and training that thought, study, skill, money and effort can give them.

There are several problems facing our people at the present time in our school affairs. The first is, equal school privileges for all children of school age. About one-third of the sum necessary for maintaining the common schools of Maine is furnished from the State treasury. While it is true that forty-seven per cent. of the towns receive a receipt in full for their State taxes, and, in addition, a check for the balance due on funds apportioned, yet there are certain considerations which it would seem have not received their merited weight in this matter of providing equal educational opportunities for all the children of the State. No other equal population in this country has furnished so large a body of men and women who have been leaders in all fields of human activity as has been found here in the State of Maine. These results have been due to several efficient causes. Our people are fortunate in having a quality of blood which makes it natural for them to be ambitious of holding places of trust and rendering a service of worth. It has also kept active within them the desire to attain distinction because of merit. The homes of Maine have been domestic universities, in which those stalwart qualities are found which characterize persons of intelligent will, enduring energy, conspicuous mental ability, fine moral quality and conquering effort. Chores and testing responsibilities have bred in our young people the wish to be, a love for work, a determination to achieve, and the courage which refuses to recognize obstacles. The sacrifices which have been made by parents and children that the boys and girls might go to the academy and then on to college, have helped in fitting these same boys and girls for stations of trust. These experiences have developed in them the capacity to meet emergencies, and the power to solve trying problems and to reach decisions for which there was no precedent. The drudging toil, the pinching economy, the struggle for subsistence, the effort necessary to insure advancement, have all been school-masters in the training of those who have given our State its quality and other states their sanest clergymen, most successful teachers, soundest jurists, ablest statesmen, wisest captains of industry and greatest poets. No true son or daughter of Maine will permit, if possible to prevent, the dimming of the lustre which these men and women have made a part of our proud inheritance. We rejoice in the work they did, the service they rendered, the results they achieved, and the glory which is theirs and ours.

We shall be wise if we learn the lesson, so clearly taught by history, that the machinery so useful in yesterday's living cannot be used in to-day's work. What was sufficient for days that are gone will not serve in the day in which we live. We have passed beyond our pioneer period. We are living in the day when the burden of each must be the concern of all. In the old days of isolation, man was not his brother's keeper in the sense he must be in these days when all communities are neighbors and the most distant often sit at our hearthstone. The electric car, the steam railroad, the telegraph, the newspaper, the magazine, make intimate companions of those who live miles apart. Frequent change of location has become a part of the progress of our era. The boy bred upon the farm comes to one of the centres of population to dig out for himself a place in the community in which he makes his new home. The dweller in the city goes back to his ancestral acres to rebuild the old home in more stately form, and brings into this rural community the enlightening and ennobling elements of urban life. He brings its culture, refinement, love of the beautiful, the desire for those things which are best—those things which stimulate and inspire and give grace and beauty to life. He brings a broader horizon into clearer skies. He brings the latest thought, the newest invention, the touch with the world, and stirs those with whom he comes in contact to a better thought and a wider vision; to a desire to know, a capacity to enjoy, a recognition of the usefulness of comeliness. This intercourse gives us a common interest in all children born within the State. We have a common concern about the character of the homes from which they come, the quality of the schools in which they are trained, and the worth and strength it is possible for them to attain.

It is the best judgment of those who have made the most careful studies of the subject, that a large majority of our citizens are willing to bear their full share of the burden imposed by the State in providing for the expenses incident to the management of its affairs and the maintaining of the institutions under its control. Citizens possessed of wealth, as a rule, are disposed to recognize that they are safer in their person, securer in their property, if suitable schools are provided for the children, if convenient roads are maintained as highways of travel, if public institutions are supported in such a way as to furnish the protection and care needed by the unfortunate, and if all the functions of government are so discharged as to hold the vicious in subjection and encourage the virtuous in their labors. The administration of all these interests involves the expenditure of large sums of money. If this is wisely done and the burden is equitably distributed among those who are protected and benefited, then each can contribute his share without hardship to himself.

EQUAL SCHOOL PRIVILEGES.

There are many advantages in being born in a rural community. The simplicity of country life makes it possible for those enjoying its benefits to grow into the possession of unusual powers. There are certain disadvantages incident to city life. The distractions of the street, the fascinations of entertainment, the absence of home cares and duties which develop resolute fibre, and the enervating contact which brushes the bloom from youth and takes the zest out of young life, are to be reckoned with in the care and training of children. Much of the best blood found in our population has come from the farm homes. That it should come flowing in the veins of cultured men and women is of vital interest to those who make up the population of our cities. A large proportion of the profitable trade of the cities is found in the rural communities. All students of industrial affairs are aware that it is the educated person who demands a home with all the conveniences and adornments of modern life. The citizen who has had the best training demands the best environment. If those who are now living in our cities are to find for themselves congenial homes in our country towns, they must go among a people fitted by culture and desire to be not only their companions but their peers. If these considerations have in them aught of merit, then all our people have a common interest in furnishing equal school privileges for all the school children of the State. The boy who lives at the end of a tote-path should have an opportunity to learn to read, write and cipher, at the expense of his parents and the parents of the boy who lives on the aristocratic street of the metropolis. They have an equal financial investment in this youth, and they should be held responsible for such schooling as will make him largely useful in whatever work he may undertake or station he may fill. The time has come when narrow-visioned selfishness should give place to broad ideas of civic duty. We can no longer attempt to settle this question by determining what we imagine will be our present money gain. We must be just and, if it be necessary, we must be generous. Those who are favored with large possessions must meet like men the responsibility which wealth places upon them. The widow's son must have an equal chance with the millionaire's boy in the struggle not only for existence but for usefulness. The wise man of wealth knows that what he invests in this boy multiplies his dollars and keeps them at par. It is as true of the State as of the individual that it cannot do the best for the humblest of its citizens without doing the best for the best conditioned of its people. Whatever helps those in need of assistance helps infinitely more those who give this aid. All questions are, in their last analysis, moral questions. Those who fail to meet moral responsibilities worthily, must suffer certain deterioration.

EXPENDITURE OF PUBLIC FUNDS.

Circumstances have made it necessary for the people of Maine to be frugal, both in their private expenses and public expenditures. While our State is found near the top in the list of the wealthy states of the Union, yet we have never had a large number of citizens who were possessed of great holdings. Our wealth has been evenly distributed, and for that reason habits of thrift have been cultivated and strict economy has been necessary. We have gained the strength and capacity which comes from acquiring property, and we have developed the wisdom and sagacity which results from careful investment. Large inheritances are not always a blessing and sometimes they are an injury to those receiving them. Things won by our own efforts are worth more than they will bring in the market. They give not only security against want, but ability to do still more and better work. The thought, care, struggle, study, effort, necessary to accumulate worldly goods breed in their possessor the power to labor, the ability to think, the desire to acquire, the self-respect which ownership gives and the dignity which follows the mastery of trying conditions.

Our citizens have long been noted for their ability to wring more than a subsistence from what has been termed "a sour and unwilling soil." They have done this because of the strength they have brought to their work, the brains they have put into it, and the faithfulness with which they have devoted themselves to it. That they have been successful there can be no question. That they have merited these successes there can be no doubt. That they are enjoying the fruit of their labors in well conditioned homes, many schools of rare merit, public institutions of a high grade, and a people of the noble quality, goes without the saying. Mistakes have been made in the over zealousness with which some have struggled to enlarge their bank accounts and multiply their acres. That this is true is not strange or discouraging. The time has come when another phase of this question must receive more careful attention than has been given it up to the present time, if our prosperity is to increase rather than to diminish. We have been intelligent and successful in our efforts to produce and accumulate. We have not always been wise in the expenditure of these accumulations. We have not been sufficiently concerned about getting a dollar's worth of service or material, or doing a dollar's worth of good with the dollar spent. In school matters we have not even exercised that prudence which has characterized the management of our private affairs. We have paid more for material furnished than it sold for in the open market, and too often we have been content with short measure, under weight, or inferior quality. Any one who spends a dollar without getting for it an adequate return, wrongs both himself and the person to whom it is paid. He wrongs himself because the possession of the dollar places upon him the responsibility of its intelligent and honest expenditure. He wrongs the person to whom it is paid because he assists in developing in him a dishonest spirit, and doing something which is infinitely worse, destroying his self-respect.

One who receives a dollar without giving for it its equivalent, either is content to be dishonest, or lives under the stinging accusation which in the end will work his corruption.

While many of these statements may .seem to have a general application, still the special purpose in introducing them at this time is to call the attention of school officials, teachers and parents, to the necessity of so conducting all the business administration of the school as to teach the important and wholesome lesson that it is as necessary to spend money honestly, as to acquire it by honest means; that possession carries with it certain duties; that the same care should be used in spending the money belonging to the public as prudent people exercise in the expenditure of their private funds, and that these principles should be exemplified in every transaction to which school officials are parties. It is a part of the business of the school to teach by its administration and by its instruction the necessity and the righteousness of thrift, economy, prudence, forethought and honesty, in the acquiring and disbursing of private and public funds.

The study which was made of the waste existing in the management of our schools, some years since, puts beyond all question the necessity for school officials giving much attention to this important subject. While there is no disposition to urge an unwise curtailing of appropriations or a niggardly expenditure of school moneys, still it is important that all those having charge of such funds shall so use them as to leave their custodians with clear consciences and bring to them the approval of honest and intelligent citizens.

LOCAL SELF-GOVERNMENT.

Local self-government has been one of the privileges highly prized by the citizens of Maine. It has been a vital factor in our growth. It has given our people a certain independence and capacity which have made them so exceptionally useful in the important walks of life. While many mistakes have been made, yet even these blunders have been the means of helping communities to grow into better conditions. Any community having the responsibility of caring for its poor, constructing its roads, and maintaining its schools, must learn its lessons in the expensive school of experience. These lessons will not be fully learned until much time has been consumed and large sums of money have apparently been wasted. Unwise methods will be used in caring for the unfortunate; unsuitable material and improper treatment of the same will be used in building highways; too large sums will be paid for material used in the school, and teachers of inferior grade will be employed to take charge of the instruction of the children. While all these items are conceded, yet it is nevertheless true that the training which comes to people from being brought together in annual town meeting and being furnished an opportunity to devise ways and means, discuss plans and projects, and decide upon policies to be adopted, is worth all it costs. It stimulates a majority of the citizens to think, study, read, consider, estimate, weigh, decide and then carry their decisions into effect. It is this training which has made our people ambitious to take positions of responsibility and furnished them with the power which enables them to fill these places with distinction. It is the school in which have been trained our independent,. thoughtful, self-respecting, hardy, capable farmers, lawyers, physicians, teachers, business men, scholars, authors, inventors, statesmen; in fact, those of every class and kind. who have been true to themselves and. helpful to others.

Local self-government has been a means of grace to our people and. should be jealously guarded, and any attempt to deprive them of this university should be met with the opposition necessary to defeat the movement. It would be well for us, however, not to be carried away by the clamor which excites alarm, when no occasion for anxiety exists. There has never been a time in the history of the State when the affairs of the town were more completely under the control of the residents of the municipality than during the past decade. While it is true that the district system has been abolished, yet it is well to bear in mind that many towns at the present time have not as large a school population as many districts had fifty years ago. While the unit of control has been changed, the extent of control has not been diminished. It is still the duty of the town to elect school officials, and to give such instructions and directions as it sees fit. Any failure on the part of these officials to comply with the wishes of the people, may be followed by the dismissal of these officers at the next town meeting. School officers are quite as likely to err in being too sensitive to the sometimes violently expressed wishes of. factions found in towns as they are to refuse to carry out the wishes of the majority. It is well to bear in mind that the town elects. its school officers, that through these officials it has charge of its teaching force, determines the subjects in which instruction shall be given, the length of time for which schools shall be maintained and through this. agency controls every item and detail connected with the administration and management of the local schools. It is not necessary to remark that the State establishes certain minimum conditions which must be complied with provided the town wishes to receive its proportion of what is known as the Common School Fund.

The law passed a few years since, authorizing towns to unite for the purpose of employing a superintendent of schools, in no way takes from the powers or in any form limits the duties and responsibilities of the citizens of the town. Under this law, school committees are elected in the same way as under the former, and they are given the same powers. The superintendent has neither more nor less of authority than under the general statute. He is elected for the same length of time, according to the same forms and discharges his duties under the same limitations as if he were the superintendent of a single town. The entering upon this arrangement depends upon the vote of the town. The power to continue in it must come from the same source. The town is at liberty to withdraw whenever a majority of the voters see fit to do so. In no way is the town relieved, or excused, or limited in the control of its schools if it takes advantage of this law.

While it is true that local self-government is a privilege to be highly prized, carefully guarded and intelligently used, and while it is also true that it furnishes the best means yet devised by man for permitting a certain kind of necessary training, yet it is also well for us not to forget that many unfortunate things will be done. We may, however, remember, with some satisfaction, that growth, to an extent, depends upon mistakes, and that experience has taught us that it is better for us to have the responsibility and make the blunders and grow into better things, than to have those affairs which concern us most vitally, managed by others and have no so-called errors made. In the one case growth is possible; in the other, degeneration in certain.

But perhaps the greatest blessing coming to the schools because of local self-government, is the local interest which will be developed in the local school. When the parent assists in the enlarging and grading of the school grounds, the providing of a suitable fence to enclose it, the erecting of safe out-buildings, the tinting or papering of schoolroom walls and ceilings, the supplying of books for the general reading of his children, and pictures for their culture and pleasure, he will be doing something more than doing all these things; he will be making a stronger, nobler, cleaner man of himself. One cannot be interested in good things without becoming better. One cannot help others without doing much for himself. One cannot serve without being served.

Experience has taught us that it is not best for the towns to furnish the means for doing the things indicated above. The work done by the School Improvement Leagues makes it clear that it is best that these things be supplied by the residents of the communities in which they are provided, to the end that the schoolroom may be the social, literary and art centre of the community in which it is located. When all our citizens are ready so to consider it, and are willing to help so to make it, then we shall have a local sentiment which will make not only the local school better but local self-government will be vindicated and local control will be assured.